GLOBAL TRADE IN THE MODERN WORLD

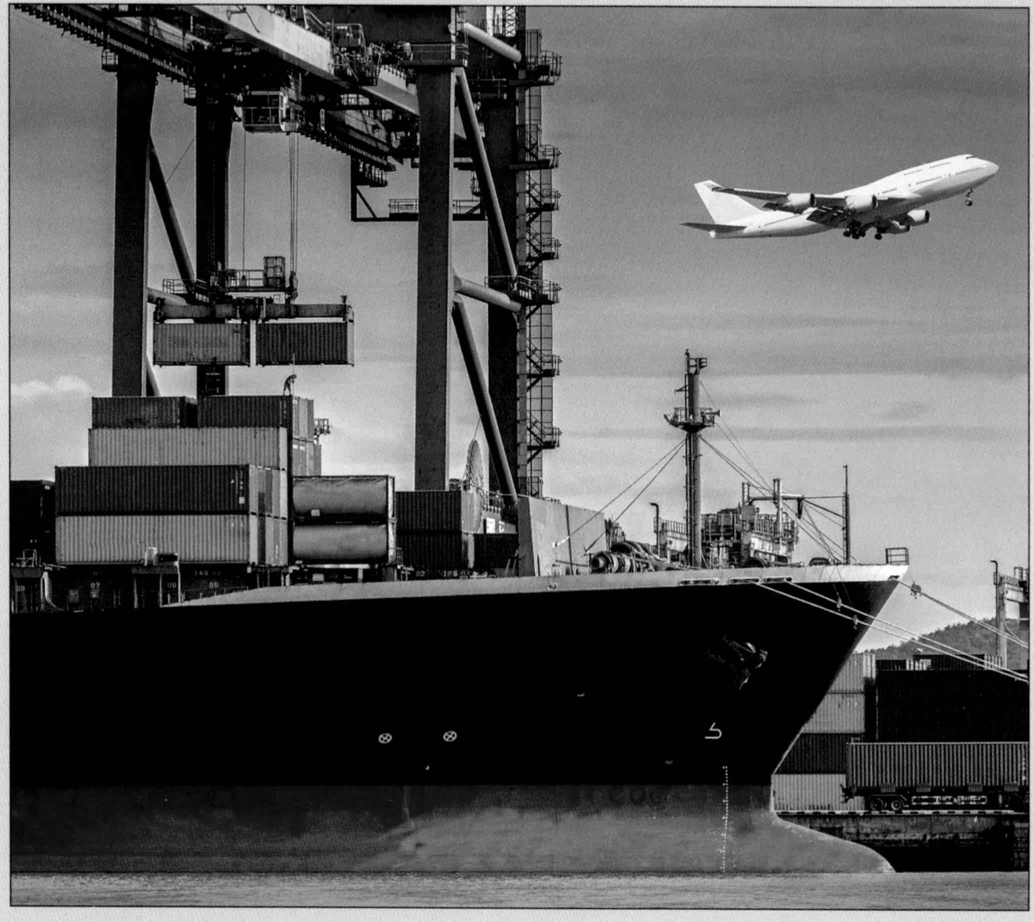

THE ECONOMICS OF GLOBAL TRADE

THE GLOBAL COMMUNITY: TECHNIQUES & STRATEGIES OF TRADE

THE GLOBAL ECONOMY AND THE ENVIRONMENT

GLOBAL INEQUALITIES AND THE FAIR TRADE MOVEMENT

GLOBAL TRADE IN THE ANCIENT WORLD

GLOBAL TRADE IN THE MODERN WORLD

GLOBAL TRADE ORGANIZATIONS

UNDERSTANDING GLOBAL TRADE & COMMERCE

GLOBAL TRADE IN THE MODERN WORLD

Laura Helweg

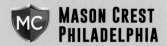

MASON CREST
PHILADELPHIA

Mason Crest
450 Parkway Drive, Suite D
Broomall, PA 19008
www.masoncrest.com

Printed and bound in the United States of America.

CPSIA Compliance Information: Batch #CWI2016.
For further information, contact Mason Crest at 1-866-MCP-Book.

First printing
1 3 5 7 9 8 6 4 2

Library of Congress Cataloging-in-Publication Data

on file at the Library of Congress
ISBN: 978-1-4222-3667-3 (hc)
ISBN: 978-1-4222-8122-2 (ebook)

Understanding Global Trade and Commerce series ISBN: 978-1-4222-3662-8

Table of Contents

KEY ICONS TO LOOK FOR:

Words to Understand: These words with their easy-to-understand definitions will increase the reader's understanding of the text, while building vocabulary skills.

Sidebars: This boxed material within the main text allows readers to build knowledge, gain insights, explore possibilities, and broaden their perspectives by weaving together additional information to provide realistic and holistic perspectives.

Research Projects: Readers are pointed toward areas of further inquiry connected to each chapter. Suggestions are provided for projects that encourage deeper research and analysis.

Text-Dependent Questions: These questions send the reader back to the text for more careful attention to the evidence presented there.

Series Glossary of Key Terms: This back-of-the book glossary contains terminology used throughout this series. Words found here increase the reader's ability to read and comprehend higher-level books and articles in this field.

People line up in front of an Apple Store in Toronto, Canada, waiting for the newest iPhones to go on sale. Apple is one of the world's most valuable companies, valued at more than $520 billion in 2016.

1

The Global Marketplace

In a one-year period ending in September 2015, Apple sold over 231 million iPhones. While Apple develops the overall design, the software, and the main operating chip in California, the iPhone is a global product. The device is a collection of materials and labor from around the world. Apple has 785 iPhone suppliers (companies that make or assemble parts) in thirty countries. Most of these are in Asia. The Asian continent hosts 662 companies that manufacture iPhone parts and assemble the final devices. Other suppliers are based in the United States (sixty), Canada (one), and Europe (forty-three). A few more suppliers are scattered across Central America, Africa, and the Middle East.

Apple uses a complex ***global supply chain***. The company sources materials, manufactures parts, and assembles products wherever the cost is lowest. The rare-earth minerals used in the iPhone's color screen, speakers, and circuitry are mined in Africa and China. Plants in Korea and Taiwan produce iPhone memory chips. The gyroscope, which allows users to flip the display, comes from factories in France and Italy. Japanese companies manufacture the cameras and screens. The fingerprint technology, touch ID sensor, and cases are produced in Taiwan (a country that is also known as Chinese Taipei).

Yet Apple uses US suppliers, too. A plant in Austin, Texas manufactures semiconductors. The glass screen is made by a Kentucky company. And an Arizona firm produces screen covers. Companies in New York, Colorado, and California make the phone's computer chips.

Most of these parts are shipped to China. Chinese workers assemble 85 percent of all iPhones. In 2014, Apple's two top suppliers each made 25 million iPhone 6s. Apple chooses Asia for the majority of iPhone production because of this capacity for high output. The company also prefers the quick response of Asian companies when Apple

Words to Understand in This Chapter

consumer—a person who buys goods and services.

export—a product or service from one country that is sold in another country.

global supply chain—the processes used to produce and distribute a product or service around the world.

globalization—the system of international connections among workers, investors, products, and consumers.

gross domestic product (GDP)—the total value of goods and services produced in a nation.

transportation—the act of moving things and people from one place to another.

changes plans. For example, before the first iPhone launched in 2007, Apple executives estimated that the company needed 8,700 engineers to manage the manufacturing process. American analysts predicted the hiring process would take nine months. Chinese suppliers filled all those positions in fifteen days. With over 32 million unemployed workers in China, there is no shortage in the labor force. By the same token, Apple says the United States does not have enough workers with the mid-level skills the iPhone's production requires.

Did You Know?

In 2007, just weeks before the Apple iPhone was scheduled to arrive in stores, Apple's CEO decided that the device needed a glass screen. American companies said the deadline was impossible. But a Chinese firm developed the screen in time. Before the deadline arrived, eight thousand employees were placing the new screens in the phone casings.

Finally, after factory workers assemble the parts and snap on the aluminum cases, the phones journey across oceans and continents. They arrive at stores and warehouses in eighteen countries. The end of the iPhone supply chain includes shipping companies, warehouse workers, and sales associates. In all, the iPhone supports millions of jobs worldwide. The device funds the wages of Apple employees, suppliers' office and factory workers, ***transportation*** workers, retail store workers, and app creators.

These jobs produce income for the nations that host Apple suppliers. The iPhone 6 release in 2014 caused a 5 percent increase in Japan's electronics ***exports***. Taiwan's electronics exports increased by 8.6 percent. Japan also profited by selling $1.17 billion in machine tools to Chinese factories producing the iPhone 6. When customers in Vancouver or Miami purchase Apple iPhones, they're supporting workers across the globe.

The Growth of Global Trade

For centuries, goods have traveled across the world to eager customers. During the Renaissance period, Europeans bought Indonesian spices, African gold, and Caribbean sugar. The Chinese purchased Peruvian silver. Africans coveted European textiles. And New World colonists enjoyed French wine and Chinese silk.

Yet the production of these goods and the transportation systems used to get them to market differed from the supply chains of today. In the Renaissance, merchants traveled long distances to get high-priced luxury items, such as spices, sugar, and silk. These products were harvested and produced near each material's source. Then they were shipped to other parts of the world in their final form, ready for purchase. The Caribbean sugar plantations are one example. Workers grew sugarcane plants, extracted the sugar from the plants, and refined the sugar on the plantation. When workers had completed every step, the refined sugar was shipped across the Atlantic to European dinner tables.

Transporting goods around the world also took more time in the Renaissance than it does today. In the 1500s, it took a full year for European merchants to sail around

China's Economic Revolution

Today, China exports more products than any other country. But for most of its history, China played a minor role in the world market. Until the twentieth century, the Chinese did not view trade as a way to gain wealth. According to traditional Chinese ideas, commercial activity lowered morals and created conflict in society. During the Renaissance period (1300–1700), China restricted foreign trade to one southern port, Canton. The Chinese rulers sought to maintain stability by limiting foreign trade.

The Canton system continued until 1912. After its reversal, conflict within the nation kept China from playing a larger part in the world economy. Trade remained low when the Communist Party took over in 1949. The communist rulers controlled the economy and focused on development within the nation. The government restricted goods coming into the country, but expanded exports.

In 1950, the United States stopped trade with China over the Korean War. This action pushed China to focus its export market on the Soviet Union. By the end of the Korean War in 1953, 75 percent of Chinese exports went to the Soviet Union, also a Communist nation. Agricultural products made up most of this amount.

After China's long-time leader, Mao Zedong, died in 1976, his successors began considering some new ideas about the national economy. The Communist government loosened its control over the economy. For the first time, it allowed private businesses to participate in international trade. Since 1979, China's income as measured by ***gross domestic product (GDP)*** has risen by an average of 8 percent every year. China has also embraced international cooperation. In 1991, China joined the Asia Pacific Economic Cooperation group. China became an official member of the World Trade Organization in 2002. In recent years, China has signed free-trade agreements with many nations in South America, Africa, Europe, and Asia.

Pedestrians crowd a shopping district in Hong Kong. In 1500, the world population was approximately 500 million people. Today, over 7 billion people live on this planet.

Africa to Indonesia, buy spices, and return to Europe. The route to China or Japan and back took even longer.

In the past five hundred years, global trade has expanded in every direction. Technology is the largest contributor to this growth. Today, machines are used to draw oil up from the ground, chop down trees, and harvest cotton. Robots process and assemble goods in factories. Airplanes carry products across oceans in a matter of hours. All these developments make trade faster and cheaper.

As a result, the world market has exploded. Industries have developed. The population has increased. These factors have combined to create a variety of products and a global demand for even the smallest goods. With the expansion of global trade, the world has become wealthier, and wealthy people buy things. During the Renaissance, only the rich could afford to purchase luxury goods. Most people struggled to pay for food, clothing, and shelter. Then the middle class appeared and expanded in the nineteenth and twentieth centuries. This group of people created a demand for all the things factories produced.

Changes in ideas and government policies have also encouraged the growth of global trade. In the past, countries approached trade by focusing on their own GDP. Today, world leaders make trade decisions based on international cooperation, the profits of companies, investors in other countries, and the living standards of people around the globe. When it comes to trade, the divisions between continents and countries have fallen away.

Globalization

This system of international connections among workers, investors, products, and buyers is called ***globalization***. Globalization connects supplies, producers, and buyers on every continent—as seen in the iPhone supply chain. This global web results in the most efficient use of the world's resources, including raw materials, labor, and finances. Globalization also leads to rapid growth in the amount of goods that are produced and traded. In turn, low-cost and high-volume production creates lower prices and more choices for ***consumers***.

Most people think of Ford as an American automobile manufacturer. However, the company has manufacturing and sales facilities in many countries, such as this one in Brasov, Romania. Similarly, "foreign" automakers like Toyota and Honda have manufacturing plants in both the United States and Canada.

The global market in the twenty-first century is interconnected as never before. All kinds of products are the result of globalization. American and Canadian families relax on Swedish furniture and watch DVDs on devices made in Japan. They sip coffee from Colombia. They wash with soap from France, drive cars made in Korea, and wear clothing stitched in Mexico. The global market is no longer a collection of products from the countries of the world. The global market is a collection of relationships and supply chains. Events in a Chinese factory affect whether a product is available in a store in Montreal. Prices go up and down with stock markets in Asia, the United States, and

Europe. When a European nation is financially unstable, the world braces for trouble.

Globalization provides many benefits. It makes more products available to consumers. It creates jobs. It connects people who speak different languages, follow different faiths, and wear different clothing.

Yet globalization has its costs. Companies that move manufacturing to the low-cost, high-labor regions of Asia leave Canadian and US workers behind. Traditional production methods, such as Indian weaving, recede as technology offers cheaper options from abroad. And some countries that play a major role in the world economy, such as China, do not always have the same values as Western nations do. Globalization is not always beneficial. But most experts agree that, overall, international trade makes the world richer, healthier, and more peaceful.

Text-Dependent Questions

1. Name three products on the global market during the Renaissance period.
2. List three benefits of globalization.

Research Project

Imagine that you own a company that sells candy bars. Make a list of your candy bar's ingredients. Then find out which country or countries produces and processes each raw material you need (such as wheat for wafers, cocoa for the chocolate coating, and aluminum foil for the wrappers). Draw a map of your candy bar's global supply chain. Use pictures to show the source of the ingredients, where they are processed and assembled, and how the finished candy bar gets to consumers.

This is a detail from a seventeenth century Portuguese map, with symbols showing the trade stations controlled by various European nations. The small ships pictured at the bottom of this map represent caravels, *sturdy vessels developed by the Portuguese that were ideal for exploration and trade.*

2

The First Age of Globalization

The modern system of global trade has its origins in the fifteenth century, as Europe was emerging from a period of isolation and economic stagnation. European rulers were interested in acquiring spices, silks, and other unusual products from foreign lands. However, the trade routes were long and dangerous, and were controlled by Muslim empires that were hostile to the Christian kingdoms of Europe. Because of this, only extremely wealthy Europeans could afford to purchase spices, such as pepper and cinnamon, because such items came from far-off lands in Asia.

During the fifteenth century, some European kingdoms began seeking sea routes that would connect their countries to the Indian Ocean and Asia. Portugal was a leader in this area. The Portuguese king, John II, paid scholars to study navigation. He instructed shipbuilders to design better vessels, called *caravels*. The Portuguese gradually explored south along the coast of Africa, establishing stations where Portuguese ships stopped and traded with the local tribes. Finally, in 1498 four Portuguese ships commanded by Vasco da Gama rounded the southern tip of Africa and sailed into the Indian Ocean, eventually landing in India and the Indonesian Spice Islands. Trading Portuguese goods he had brought, and sometimes using military force, da Gama filled his ships with Indonesian spices, Indian fabric, and African gold. He returned to Portugal in 1499 with goods that were

Words to Understand in This Chapter

comparative advantage—the ability to produce a product or service at the lowest cost, compared to the cost of other economic activity.

economist—a person who studies how goods and services are produced, sold, and bought.

gold standard—a financial system in which a nation's currency is equal to a specific amount of pure gold and the nation promises that its currency can be exchanged for gold.

import—a product or service that is bought from another country.

Industrial Revolution—a period during the eighteenth and nineteenth centuries in Europe and North America in which the introduction of powered machines increased manufacturing and added to national GDP.

investment—the act of putting out money in hopes of gaining a profit.

mercantilism—an economic system that promotes government regulation of the economy and focuses on bolstering national income.

monopoly—complete control of the supply of a good or service in a place or market, or a company that holds complete control of a good or service.

tariff—a tax on goods entering or leaving a country.

telegraph—a system of sending messages over distances with wire and electrical signals.

worth sixty times as much as his expedition had cost.

The Portuguese soon returned with warships, which they used to control the Indian Ocean during the first half of the sixteenth century. As they had on the West African coast, Portugal established trade stations at key ports on the East African Coast, in India, and on various islands. The Portuguese did not allow ships from other European countries to participate in the Indian Ocean trade. This was because of the dominant economic philosophy of the time, ***mercantilism***. The mercantile theory held that a nation's wealth depended on the amount of precious metal the nation possessed. Mercantilists thought tight control over the sale of goods in and out of a country helped build the nation's stock of gold and silver. According to this theory, a country can only gain wealth when the goods it sells are more valuable than those it must buy. This theory means that all traders are competing for a share of the same wealth. The Portuguese wanted to protect their trade routes to make sure their country had an advantage over its competitors.

Portugal's trade with Africa and Asia made it the wealthiest kingdom in Europe, and other nations soon followed its example. In 1492 Spain sent Christopher Columbus's expedition west across the Pacific Ocean hoping to find a sea route to Asia. Columbus wound up discovering islands in North America. During a subsequent voyage, Columbus would discover the South American continent. He claimed these lands for Spain. Other European powers, such as Great Britain, France, and the Netherlands, would soon follow the Spanish west across the Atlantic, claiming lands in North America as their own and establishing colonies.

Both the British and the Dutch also sought profitable trade with Asia. In 1577, navigator Francis Drake headed west from Plymouth, England, with five ships. Britain and Spain were at war at this time, so Drake intended to attack Spanish colonies and shipping in South America and Central America. He also wanted to establish an English trade route to the Indian Ocean. Drake wound up sailing around the world, returning to England in 1580. His ships were loaded with captured Spanish silver and goods seized from Portuguese ships, as well as cloves and nutmeg he had purchased in the Spice Islands.

In 1600, the English crown created the English East India Company to manage trade and govern English trade stations in the Indian Ocean. Soon, England was managing a busy trade network in the East Indies.

Meanwhile, the Dutch also sailed into the Indian Ocean. Before 1580, the Dutch had purchased spices from the Portuguese. But that year, the Spanish king claimed Portugal as part of his expanding empire and banned Dutch merchants from the country. Soon afterward, a Dutch expedition sailed around Africa to purchase spices at their source. In 1602, the Dutch government created the Dutch East India Company to control Dutch trade in the Indian Ocean.

For the first half of the seventeenth century, the Netherlands was the dominant trading power of Europe.

To protect British trade, warships sometimes attacked merchant ships from rival countries. These Chinese ships are being destroyed by a warship owned by the British East India Company.

From their base in Batavia, Indonesia, the Dutch traded with China and Japan. Chinese tea and silk, Japanese metals, Indonesian spices, and Indian cotton all moved through Batavia. The Dutch traded these goods throughout Asia. The highest-quality products they shipped home.

England had been troubled by religious and political turmoil at home, but after the English Civil War ended in 1651 the nation could refocus on trade. English ships soon ventured to China. There they exchanged Indian cotton, watches, and silver for Chinese tea. Soon English merchants had developed their own strong trade network within Asia.

Like other mercantilist nations, England tried to shield its trade from competition. The Navigation Acts prevented foreign ships from landing in English ports carrying foreign goods. Other laws protected English industries by restricting ***imports***, goods bought from other countries. For example, a 1678 law banned the import of French silk and linen to protect England's textile industry.

New World, New Markets

The sixteenth century was an age of colonization by Europeans. Spain conquered the Aztec and Inca peoples, gaining control over large areas of Mexico and Peru. The Spanish colonies soon began sending valuable products, such as silver and sugar, back to Spain. Other nations followed their example. Portugal took control of Brazil. France explored and settled Canada. Great Britain established colonies along the Atlantic coast of North America, as well as some Caribbean islands.

The New World colonies supplied Europe with inexpensive raw materials and food. The vast lands produced a variety of agricultural goods. The colonies nourished Europe with corn, wheat, coffee, and sugar. These products replaced spices as the most widely traded commodities after 1700.

The colonies, in turn, provided a new market for their home countries. Spain increased its production of oil, grains, fruits, and livestock to please its hungry colonists. France sent food, wine, and silk to its western colonies. England kept homemade goods cheap in the colonies by keeping ***tariffs***, or taxes on imports, low.

European nations viewed the New World colonies as businesses that should generate incomes. Accordingly, the governments passed laws to boost profits from those colonies. One common colonial trade law was a ban on trade with other nations. American colonists could only sell sugar, tobacco, rice, cotton, wool, and furs to England or to another British colony. And they could not buy goods from outside the British Empire. Governments also prevented colonies from producing goods that would compete with the home country's industries. For example, England prohibited American production of cloth to protect the English textile industry. Furthermore, only the home countries were allowed to sell colonial products to other nations. The business of re-exporting goods from the colonies to China and India turned London into a major financial center.

However, trade restrictions led to tension in some colonies. Such tension in Britain's thirteen North American colonies led to cries for independence and the American Revolution in 1775. Similarly, resistance to trade restrictions in Saint-Domingue eventually led Haiti to declare independence from France in 1804.

Changing Economic Theories

As the colonial system was thriving in the eighteenth century, some European thinkers began to question the theory of mercantilism. One of the first to do this was a British ***economist*** named Henry Martyn. In his 1701 book *Considerations Upon the East India Trade,* Martyn argued that the amount of things people purchased was a better indicator of the true level of national wealth than was a storehouse full of gold or silver:

> Cloaths and Manufactures are real and principal riches. Are not these things esteem'd Riches over the World? And that Country thought richest which most abounds in them? Holland [the Netherlands] is the Magazin [store] of every Country's Manufactures; English Cloth, French Wines, Italian Silks, are treasur'd up there. If these things were not riches, they wou'd not give their [money] for 'em.

Later in the 18th century, the Scottish economist Adam Smith agreed with Martyn's conclusions. Smith believed that trade regulations "may, I think, be demonstrated to be in every case a complete piece of dupery, by which the interests of the State and the nation is constantly sacrificed to that of some particular class of traders." By traders, Smith meant producers and merchants. For example, a farmer who grew corn benefited from import restrictions on grain. Trade controls, Smith said, favored only a small group of citizens. He believed that tariffs and other trade limits robbed the nation as a whole of the profits that free

International Currency Exchange

Today, countries all over the world use the US dollar in trade exchanges. In the sixteenth through the nineteenth century, the Spanish dollar, or "piece of eight," was the most commonly used currency. The Spanish dollar's dominance corresponded to a silver mining boom in the Spanish colonies of the Americas. Silver mints in Mexico and Peru created the dollar by stamping an ounce of silver with symbols of the Spanish crown. The Spanish dollars made their way around the world through the global trading networks of the European imperial powers.

A shipwreck discovered off the Australian coast in 1963 demonstrates the reach of the global trade network in the seventeenth century. The wreck also shows the dominance of the Spanish piece of eight. The *Vergulde Draek* had belonged to the Dutch East India Company. It had sailed from the Netherlands in 1655, but sank near Australia the next year. The *Vergulde Draek*'s hull held thousands of silver coins. The ship had been carrying Spanish pieces of eight, originally minted in Mexico City, to the Dutch trading post at Batavia. The Dutch had planned to use the money to purchase valuable trade goods to bring back to Europe.

trade would provide. In 1776, Smith published his ideas in a book called *The Wealth of Nations*.

Smith also criticized ***monopolies***, such as the East India Company. The English government prohibited merchants outside of the company from trading in specific goods, such as cloth and tea. The company had no competition in these areas. Therefore, the East India Company could charge high prices. But government's job, Smith argued, was to take care of its people. Allowing citizens to purchase goods from the lowest-priced seller was part of that responsibility. When governments restricted trade, Smith argued, they meddled with fair competition. The lack of competition increased prices.

About 50 years later, an English political economist David Ricardo used Smith's economic theories to attack the Corn Laws, a set of tariffs that increased the price of grain imported into the United Kingdom. The tariffs allowed landowners to charge inflated prices for their grain while still undercutting the expensive imports. This led to unbearably high food prices for England's poor.

The Wealth of Nations, *by Adam Smith, is considered a pioneering guide to economics and free market enterprise.*

Ricardo argued that the Corn Laws were damaging England's economy.

In addition to opposing the Corn Laws, David Ricardo opposed all import restrictions. Ricardo believed that all nations would profit from free trade, even nations with fewer resources than others. He illustrated this idea with an example: suppose it took 100 people one year to produce a unit of cloth in England. It also took 120 English subjects one year to produce a unit of wine. Now suppose that in Portugal, it took only 90 people to produce a unit of cloth, and it took 80 Portuguese workers to produce a unit of wine. In this case, Portugal has an absolute advantage in both cloth and wine production because fewer workers can produce the same amount. However, Ricardo argued, England has a ***comparative advantage*** in cloth production, because Portugal's profits would be the highest if its workforce focused on producing wine, which it could sell to England, while purchasing cloth from England. Therefore, Ricardo concluded, all countries could succeed in an open market.

Britain Leads the Way

These ideas about free trade had begun to take hold in Britain by the start of the nineteenth century. At that time, Britain led the world as an industrial, financial, and naval power. The British Empire included land on each of the six inhabited continents. And it had survived the independence of the United States. In fact, Britain had a strong trading partner in the new nation. Between 1788 and 1798, the value of British exports to the United States tripled.

In 1821, Britain established a ***gold standard***. The nation tied the value of its currency, the pound sterling, to gold. One pound sterling was worth 0.24 ounces (6.8 g) of pure gold. The gold standard made the pound the world's most stable and valuable currency. These strengths made overseas purchases cheap for British investors. In view of these advantages, other European nations and the United States adopted the gold standard in the 1870s. All at once the value of these nation's currencies held steady in relation to one another. The gold standard removed the risk of foreign ***investment*** among nations using this standard.

Britain also led the world in reducing trade barriers. In 1833, Parliament allowed the charter of the East India Company to expire. The company had operated for more than two hundred years. Once the charter ran out, other merchants could sell Indian cloth, Chinese tea, and other previously monopolized products. The company's demise signaled the beginning of a focus on free trade in Europe.

Next, Parliament repealed the Corn Laws in 1846. The tariff's removal made imported grain inexpensive. As a result, the cost of food in England fell dramatically. Britain switched its efforts from producing grain to producing manufactured goods, such as clothing, dishes, books, and clocks. British industries adopted new technology and increased manufacturing production. Workers moved from fields to factories. The ***Industrial Revolution*** began in England during the last quarter of the eighteenth century and soon spread to Canada, the United States, and the rest of Europe.

Nineteenth-century improvements in transportation, such as railroads and steamships, made it easier to move trade goods to different markets.

From 1801 to 1901, British manufacturing output increased twelvefold. British goods dominated the world marketplace.

The biggest change to the world trade climate in the nineteenth century came in 1860. That year, British politician Richard Cobden made a trade agreement with French statesman Michel Chevalier. The Cobden-Chevalier Treaty greatly lowered tariffs between the two countries. The treaty also contained a clause specifying that no other country could obtain lower tariffs from either nation. The Most Favored Nation clause required that if any trade agreement made with a third country lowered a tariff below the amount set between Britain and France, the British or French tariff for that product would go down to the same amount.

The success of the Cobden-Chevalier Treaty inspired other European nations to make similar tariff-reducing agreements. The new treaties often included Most Favored Nation clauses. As the number of treaties increased and as nations fulfilled Most Favored Nation clauses, Europe and its colonies formed a trading zone nearly free of trade barriers.

The Industrial Revolution

As goods flowed freely among European nations and their colonies, technology changed the amount and kinds of goods being traded. During the Industrial Revolution, production of manufactured goods increased. The higher output lowered prices.

In England, improvements in technology multiplied cloth production by one hundred times. The cotton gin increased the amount of cotton fiber that could be processed. As a result, cotton plantations supplied textile mills with more raw materials. Because of steam technology, the mills operated more efficiently and produced more cloth. All these developments caused the cost of fabric to plummet.

As factories churned out more products, transportation technology made getting goods from one country to another cheaper than ever. By the late 1830s, steamships regularly crossed the Atlantic Ocean. After the first steam-powered railroad appeared in England in 1821, tracks crisscrossed continents. The US transcontinental railroad was completed in 1869. Workers finished the Canadian-Pacific transcontinental railroad in 1885. These lines connected inland production facilities with coastal ports.

Advancements in inland water travel also connected producers to markets. The Erie Canal, completed in 1825, linked the US agricultural center—the Midwest—to New York and the Atlantic Ocean. Likewise, the Suez Canal, finished in 1869 in Egypt, bridged the Mediterranean Sea and the Red Sea. This 102-mile (164-km) canal eliminated the route around Africa to reach the Indian Ocean. Before the canal, steamships could not travel from Europe to Asia because the African route required more coal than the ships could carry. The Suez Canal marked the replacement of sailing ships with steamships in commercial transportation.

Another innovation added fresh food to the world market. Refrigeration by ice blocks was first developed in the 1830s. By 1870 US ranchers sent meat to Europe. A decade later, refrigerated ships traveled to Europe from as far away as Brazil and Australia. The ability to keep food cool connected the meat industries in these countries to large European populations.

The invention of the ***telegraph*** brought markets even closer together. A telegraph message crossed the Atlantic Ocean for the first time in 1858. Before that, producers and purchasers in America and Europe had to wait ten days to learn the prices of goods on the other side of the Atlantic. Ten days was the length of an Atlantic crossing by steamship. By contrast, the telegraph carried market information in a matter of seconds.

The explosion of transportation and communication technology in the nineteenth century drove down prices. The lower prices increased consumer demand as more people could afford to buy small luxuries. Overseas trade helped fuel the Industrial Revolution by expanding the consumer market.

Free Trade's Winners and Losers

Open markets led to better products and lower prices around the world. But not everyone benefited from global competition. European farmers struggled when food prices fell due to cheap crops coming from the New World. As a result, many farmers left the countryside and began to work in city factories.

The way the world market worked in the nineteenth century confirms an idea developed by two economists in 1941. Wolfgang Stolper and Paul Samuelson came up with the Stolper-Samuelson Theorem to explain why some countries support free trade and some do not. According to the theorem, nations with scarce land, labor, or funds support trade restrictions that protect their limited resources. However, nations with lots of land, labor, or funds support free trade because they have the advantage in the marketplace.

Based on the patterns of trade in the nineteenth century, the theorem seems to be correct. During that period, the United States was rich in land. Britain was rich in workers and funds. In accord with Stolper-Samuelson, US landowners and British laborers and investors favored free trade. On the other hand, the United States was low on funds and labor. Britain was low on land. Therefore, investors and workers in the United States and landowners in Britain supported trade restrictions.

Free trade in the global market also harmed poor countries. While Europe and the United States industrialized and grew rich, nations in the southern hemisphere lost their industries to the northern competition. Artisans in India, Egypt, and Mexico could not compete with the inexpensive products shipped in from Europe and North America. Southern hemisphere builders, weavers, and metalworkers were forced to leave their skilled trades. To earn money, they labored to produce the raw materials needed by the wealthy nations' manufacturing operations. The global market no longer focused on high-priced primary products, such as spices, tea, and sugar. Instead, low-priced manufactured goods, such as cookware, furniture, and machinery made up the majority of traded products. This shift put the industrialized nations of Europe and the United States in the driver's seat of the world economy.

The United States Stands Alone

Yet the United States did not join Europe in the open market in the nineteenth century. The nation put up a tariff wall between the United States and Europe's manufactured goods. The tariffs served multiple purposes: First, they allowed US manufacturers to grow and innovate without the pressures of overseas competition. Second, the tariffs supported the federal government. In the nineteenth century, the United States did not have a federal income tax. Tariffs on foreign goods made up 90 percent of the US government's budget. This dependence meant that the government had to raise import fees when the US economy per-

Slaves pick cotton on a Southern plantation, 1850s. When the Civil War began in 1861, nearly 4 million African Americans were held in slavery. Their labor fueled the South's economy, which was based on cash crops like cotton, tobacco, and rice.

formed poorly. Higher tariffs further raised prices and hurt struggling citizens.

In fact, the issue of trade protections sparked the first major dispute between the North and the South. The North was the center of manufacturing industry in the nineteenth century. Northerners favored tariff protection to shelter US factories from more established European firms. The South's economy relied primarily on agricultural production. So Southerners wanted free trade. Southerners knew that low tariffs would result in other nations keeping tariffs low on incoming Southern products. The tensions continued throughout the Civil War (1861–1865). At that time, President Abraham Lincoln raised tariffs even higher to fund the Union army. After the war, tariffs remained high to pay to rebuild the South.

World trade grew substantially in the nineteenth century. The Industrial Revolution increased production. Technology connected suppliers, producers, and buyers through improvements in transportation and communications. The Cobden-Chevalier Treaty flipped a switch in Europe, and nations across the continent stripped away trade barriers. The world's GDP rose by an average of 2.1 percent a year. World exports grew even faster, by an average of 3.4 percent a year. The world economy had become truly global, and it continued to grow.

Text-Dependent Questions

1. Name three developments in technology that advanced world trade in the nineteenth century.
2. Why did the United States refuse to join Europe in lowering tariffs in the nineteenth century?

Research Project

Choose one country in Western Europe and research what products it exported in the nineteenth century. Write a two-page report that demonstrates the reasons the selected country specialized in these products. Explore the relationships between the products and the availability of natural resources, labor, and funding in that country.

3

Destruction and Depression

Global trade increased through the end of the nineteenth century. Yet free-trade policies became less common in the final three decades of the century. One cause of new restrictions was a slump in the economy from 1873 to 1877. People had less extra money and demand for goods fell. Nations tried to protect their industries with import restrictions. In addition, trade barriers against food goods rose in the decades before 1900. These protections shielded European farmers from the cheap prices of New World agricultural products. Import prices had dropped further because of transportation improvements, and European farmers could not compete without restrictions. Finally, European nations raised tariffs to strengthen colonial economies.

Although tariffs rose from 1880 to 1914, total world trade actually tripled. In part, shrinking transportation costs made up for rising tariffs. In 1914, another cost-saving canal, this time in Panama, made the world smaller. The shortcut through Central America shrank the shipping distance from Europe to Australia and Asia. Historians also associate the increase in trade with the huge profits of the Industrial Revolution. According to a general economic belief, wealthy societies trade more than poor societies.

World War I and Global Trade

Yet Europe's wealth was on shaky ground. Webs of opposing political alliances extended across the continent and into the colonies. These pacts made the region a dry wood pile ready to ignite at the smallest spark. When a few radicals in Bosnia murdered the heir to the Austro-Hungarian Empire in 1914, the world exploded into World War I.

Suddenly, most of the active trading nations were caught up in ***total warfare***. Economic activity shifted to the war effort. As nations focused their resources on fighting,

Words to Understand in This Chapter

Great Depression—a worldwide period of economic collapse between 1929 and 1939.

isolationism—a political policy of not being involved with other nations.

multinational corporation—a company that operates in more than one country.

stock market—a public exchange where ownership of shares in companies are bought and sold.

total warfare—a way of fighting a war that uses all of a nation's resources, including nonmilitary workers and processes.

French soldiers wait in a defensive position for a German assault, 1914. Just a few months earlier, an all-out war in Europe had seemed unthinkable. None of the continent's Great Powers had fought against another for more than 40 years. Europe enjoyed rising prosperity, driven by international trade and investment. No one envisioned that the First World War would result in more than 16 million dead and would completely redraw the world map.

they reduced exports. Factories that had produced household goods, farm equipment, and clothing for export began manufacturing weapons, military vehicles, and uniforms for the military. The drop in manufactured exports left empty spaces on store shelves around the world.

The remaining trade focused on war materials. The battling armies needed food and parts for equipment and weapons. The United States, which did not join the war until 1917, shipped arms and food to Britain and its allies. Canada, in the war as part of the British Empire, also played the role of supplier. During the war, the value of both US and Canadian exports tripled. Exports also rose in Sweden, a neutral European nation. And Chile supplied the armies with grain, meat, and copper. As the recipients of the war materials, European countries saw imports increase.

Did You Know?

The US meat industry exported ten times as much meat during World War I as it had before the war.

During the war, military barriers further hemmed in trade. In 1915, Britain prevented ships from entering Germany's North Sea ports. Germany's imports fell by over one-third. In response, German submarines attacked British vessels and US supply ships in the Atlantic Ocean. The sinking of the *Lusitania*, a British ocean liner with many Americans aboard, by a German submarine prompted many leaders in the United States to seriously consider entering the war.

Adding to the trouble, Europe abandoned the gold standard after the war started. War costs forced nations to leave the standard because the countries printed money to pay for the war. They printed more money than they had gold to back it up. Therefore, nations could no longer promise to exchange their currency for gold. The end of the gold standard cut Europe loose from the stability of gold-based exchange rates. The value of European currencies fell as nations printed more and more money to pay for the war. The British pound, the French franc, and the German mark lost most of their worth. This financial insecurity brought trade levels even lower.

When the war finally came to an end, Europe was both

physically and financially ruined. Bombs had left the buildings of Ypres, Belgium and Paris, France as piles of rubble. Trench warfare had ripped, exploded, and burned huge areas of European farmland. Not only had the war interrupted the production of exported goods, but many factories and fields had been damaged or destroyed.

The US president, Woodrow Wilson, knew that international trade needed to rebound for the world to recover. Wilson called for the "removal, so far as possible, of all economic barriers and the establishment of an equality of trade conditions." However, US politicians did not accept Wilson's vision. Congress refused to join the League of Nations, an organization that would carry out Wilson's plan for negotiating peaceful international relations.

As Wilson and other leaders had predicted, European nations struggled to resurrect their economies. They needed large sums to rebuild cities, revive peacetime manufacturing, and provide food and shelter for throngs of people displaced by battle. In addition, former soldiers needed jobs. And Germany owed Britain, France, and others $33 billion in reparations, payback for the costs of the war it had caused. The Allied nations also owed $26.5 billion to the United States for war loans. And the United States refused to lower tariffs on European goods and help Europe regain trade profits.

The Great Depression

The war had shattered the world economy, and foreign trade remained far below prewar levels. Trade restrictions made the recovery even more difficult. Many nations had increased protections during the war, and governments were slow to repeal them. In France, tariffs were four times higher after the war than before. The United States maintained its tariff wall.

To get around high import taxes, some companies opened locations in other countries to produce goods for those nations. These were the first ***multinational*** corporations, companies that operate in more than one country. In particular, US auto firms started or bought thousands of subsidiary companies in Europe, Canada, and Latin America.

Industrial production in Europe recovered to prewar levels by 1924. But nations had found other sources for goods during the war. They no longer needed goods made in Europe. The return of European products caused an oversupply in the world market, and prices dropped. Without the need to supply massive armies, food and raw material prices also declined. US farm prices fell 52 percent from 1928 to 1933. Metal and building material prices also fell by 18 percent.

Then, in October 1929 the ***stock market*** in New York City crashed. The companies represented on the stock exchange lost most of their value, and investors lost billions of dollars. Many American citizens and businesses lost all their savings. The crash led to a worldwide economic collapse, known as the ***Great Depression***. Businesses closed. People lost jobs and homes. Families struggled to pay for the basics—food, clothing, and shelter. Western consumers,

Piles of German money in a Berlin bank during the mid-1920s. Germany had borrowed large amounts of money to pay for its military expenses during World War I. When the war ended, it had no way to pay back the debt as well as the enormous fines imposed by the victorious Allied nations. As a result German currency went through a period of hyper-inflation. In 1918 an American dollar was worth about 8 German marks. By 1923, it took 800 million marks to buy one dollar's worth of goods.

who had eagerly bought the products of the Industrial Revolution, saved their coins for bread and rent. National income dropped by 25 to 30 percent in the United States, Canada, Germany, and parts of Latin America.

The drop in wealth created a plunge in demand, and world trade dwindled. By the end of 1932, world trade was at barely one-third of its 1929 level. Trade in manufactured goods declined by 42 percent. Trade in raw materials fell by 13 percent. In Canada, the value of exports slipped from $1.341 million in 1928 to less than half that, $495 million, in 1932. Total exports dropped by over 50 percent in Australia, Asia, and Latin America. The loss resulted in many Latin American countries going bankrupt.

To protect its industries from further losses, the US government raised tariffs. The 1930 Smoot-Hawley Tariff

The Upside of Free Trade

In 1857, the British politician Richard Cobden wrote: "Free trade is God's diplomacy, and there is no other certain way of uniting people in the bonds of peace." The trade treaties that Cobden negotiated began a peaceful time in European history. By contrast, World War II—the deadliest war in humanity's history to date—followed the isolation of the 1920s and 1930s. These events suggest that the opposite of Cobden's statement is also true: The absence of trade between nations increases the chance of war.

Free trade certainly has economic benefits. Yet the wealth made from trade creates additional advantages. For instance, art and culture flourish in wealthy societies. In the Renaissance, only a small group of rich citizens supported artists and musicians. Therefore, artists and musicians only created what wealthy people liked. Today, nearly anyone can listen to classical, country, hip-hop, or rock-and-roll music. Art enthusiasts enjoy creations from abstract metal statues to watercolor paintings to digital works.

The global market also connects people of different cultures. A person in Detroit, Michigan can dine at a Nigerian restaurant, read a Russian novel, or watch a Japanese cartoon. Likewise, the Japanese cartoon artist might enjoy a French croissant or a Brazilian pop song.

Yes, free trade increases wealth. It allows people to have more possessions. But its benefits extend beyond material comfort. Free trade promotes understanding of other cultures and peace among nations.

added import taxes on everything from Swiss watches to Spanish wine corks. In response, Canada, France, Italy, Spain, and Switzerland raised tariffs on US goods. Other nations followed suit. High tariffs made it even more difficult for European economies to rebound. The added taxes raised prices on European imports. This meant that European goods did not sell at the rate needed for the European countries to earn enough to pay the war debts these countries had incurred.

> **Did You Know?**
>
> In 1933, one out of every four US workers and one out of every five Canadian workers needed jobs. In Germany, over one-third of people were unemployed during the Great Depression.

The world economy was teetering on the edge of a cliff, and the major nations backed away. Nations stopped producing for the world market. Instead, they focused on meeting their own needs for food and goods. Countries found uses within their own borders for products they had been exporting. They also adapted industries to provide for their own citizens. Nations became more independent and less connected to other countries.

The value of world trade in US dollars fell by two-thirds from 1929 to 1933. This slump meant that merchants and business professionals stopped traveling across borders. Politicians stopped meeting to make trade agreements. And citizens stopped buying goods made by people from different cultures. This ***isolationism*** bred distrust of other people. Along with economic troubles, it created radical nationalist movements in Russia, Italy, and Germany. A German busi-

Unemployed men line up outside a store offering free coffee, doughnuts, and soup in Chicago. At the height of the Great Depression, roughly 25 percent of Americans were without work. Unemployment was even higher in Canada, at about 27 percent.

nessman who later joined Hitler's Nazi Party remembered the bleak days of the Depression:

> I couldn't pay my people. My assets had melted away. Once again we experienced hunger and deprivation . . . The still somewhat prosperous middle class was destroyed . . . I fled from a government that permitted such misery.

Economic hardship and isolation contributed to the prejudice and nationalist fervor that set the stage for another devastating war.

World War II consumed the global economy from 1939 to 1945. Again, the market experienced the patterns seen in World War I. Nations focused their output and funds on the war. Exports plummeted. Political and military actions cut off international relations. Once more the United States and Canada supplied the Allies of Western Europe. In 1943, war materials made up over 80 percent of US exports. And once again, when the war ended, Europe stumbled out, crippled by bombing, population loss, and debt.

Text-Dependent Questions

1. List four nations that profited from trade during World War I.
2. Describe three ways the Great Depression affected world trade.

Research Project

Canada helped supply the Allied Powers with food, machinery, and other materials during World War I. Find out more about Canada's war production and its effect on the Canadian economy. Write a 500-word speech arguing whether or not World War I economically improved the daily lives of Canadian civilians. Use specific details to support your claim.

The 1944 Bretton Woods Agreement established a system for managing the currency exchange rate of dozens of countries by pegging their value to the price of gold. This helped to stabilize these nations' economies, enabling greater trade after World War II.

A New Age of Globalization

When World War II ended in 1945, the United States was again the only world power with its economy intact. US President Harry S. Truman decided the United States should take the lead in the world-wide recovery. The United States had isolated itself following World War I. But this time US officials saw an opportunity. They wanted to lead the world back to the global market. "The main prize of a victory . . . is limited and temporary power to establish the world we want to live in," said an official report.

The Bretton Woods System

Even before the conflict came to an end, the United States invited forty-four countries to a conference in Bretton Woods, New Hampshire. The goal of the United Nations Monetary and Financial Conference of 1944 (known as the Bretton Woods Conference) was to rebuild the world economy. These nations realized that cooperation and group responsibility were the keys to reviving peace and trade. They also knew that the lack of these elements contributed to the fragile world economy after World War I and the Great Depression.

During twenty-two days in July 1944, representatives from these nations acknowledged problems and discussed solutions. First, the leaders agreed that the world needed a new financial system. The new system should avoid the instability of floating currency values. It should also stay away from the rigidity of the gold standard. In response to these concerns, the leaders created the ***par value system***. In this system, each country determined an exchange rate for its currency. The nations also pledged to maintain that value. The par value system was similar to the gold standard in several ways. First, each nation tied the value of its currency to a shared unit—the US dollar. The dollar was itself backed by gold. Thirty-five US dollars were worth one ounce (28 g) of gold.

Words to Understand in This Chapter

communism—a political and economic system based on property being publicly owned.

components—parts that make up a manufactured product.

outsourcing—the act of using workers in a different country.

par value system—a world financial system in which nations set the value of their currency in relation to the US dollar and the US dollar is tied to an amount of gold.

Representatives of more than 40 nations met at Bretton Woods, New Hampshire, in July 1944 to discuss monetary stabilization as an aid to post-war trade.

A companion problem was how to keep currencies from having big changes in value. The conference attendees created the International Monetary Fund (IMF) to address this issue. They designed the fund as a reserve bank. Nations would contribute money. Then, in times of trouble, a member nation could take out money to pay its debts instead of changing the value of its currency. The member nations would jointly govern the fund. Each nation would have a number of votes that corresponded to the size of its economy and its contribution to the fund. This arrangement gave the United States one-third of all IMF votes. With those votes came the unofficial job of world money manager. Leaders also established the World Bank to provide loans for postwar reconstruction and development.

The Bretton Woods representatives wanted to avoid the unfriendly trade policies of the 1930s, which had exacerbated the Great Depression. With US leadership, European nations decided to eliminate trade and investment barriers within Europe. This commitment was the first step toward the 1958 formation of the European Economic Community free-trade area. The organization eventually became the European Union.

The nations represented at Bretton Woods also agreed that the global market needed a setting for discussing trade issues and lowering trade barriers. In 1947, representatives from many of the same nations traveled to Geneva, Switzerland. They hoped to lower trade restrictions and develop policies for international trade. Over six months, world leaders made various bargains about traded goods, tariffs, and other trade issues. All together, these agreements lowered tariffs and other trade restrictions around the world. At the end of the conference, twenty-three nations signed the General Agreement on Tariffs and Trade (GATT). The GATT made the individual agreements official and set out rules and procedures for future trade talks.

GATT conferences became the platform for trade conversations. Eight GATT conferences took place between 1947 and 1995. In 1995, the World Trade Organization replaced the GATT system.

From 1947 until 1991, the United States and the Soviet Union waged a struggle for influence across the globe. The confrontation played out in various arenas—military, economic, diplomatic, and even cultural, dividing Europe between the communist East and the democratic West. The Berlin Wall, which divided Soviet-backed East Germany from the American-supported West Germany, was a famous symbol of Cold War tensions.

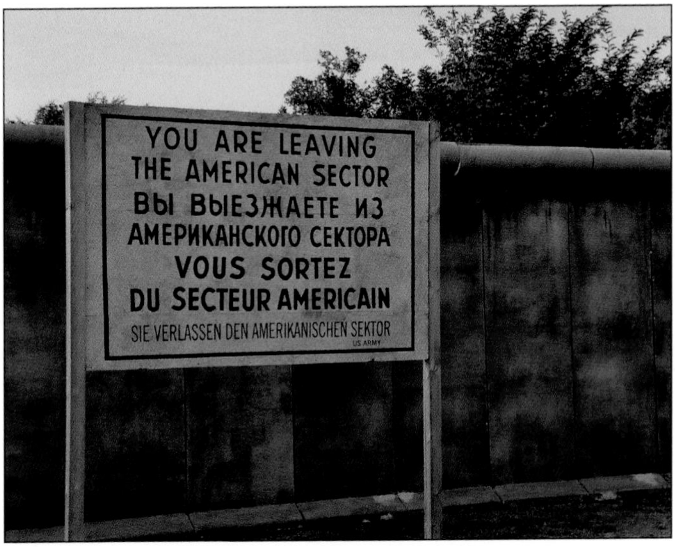

A Slow Recovery

The Bretton Woods Conference and the General Agreement on Tariffs and Trade promised stability and cooperation in the future world economy. However, the wounds of two world wars, a global depression, and isolationist policies were not easily healed. The transition period dragged on for years.

European economies recovered more slowly than anticipated. As a result, these nations struggled to repay loans from the World Bank and the United States. In addition, the original amount of money deposited into the International Monetary Fund was too low. The fund's supply was far below the amount nations needed to pay recovery costs and debts. Furthermore, the peace deals struck at the end of the war had created new nations. These countries were still organizing their governments and could not join the new agreements.

Despite these difficulties, the United States continued its commitment to leadership and to the open market. It kept tariffs on European goods low to help European industries rebuild. The United States also sent $13 billion ($130 billion in 2015 dollars) in aid to European countries through the Marshall Plan. This was a program of US financial aid to help rebuild the economies of war-torn European nations. The United States gave additional loans to nations that needed extra help. Other countries accepted the United States as the world's economic leader in exchange for policies and funds that helped them rebuild.

Meanwhile, the world divided into two groups. Under the leadership of the United States, the West promoted democracy. Under the Soviet Union, Eastern Europe, and Western Asia operated under ***communism***. Democratic countries preferred to trade with other democratic countries. Communist nations gave more trading benefits to other communist countries. During the 1950s through 1980s, in a period known as the Cold War, trade restrictions grew between democracies and communist nations.

The Modern Age

The recovery from World War II was long and difficult. Yet the value of world trade grew by over 6 percent each year from 1945 to 1995. The amount of national income from exported goods also grew. In 1945, trade made up only 5.5 percent of world GDP. By contrast, trade accounted for over 17 percent of world GDP in 1998.

The twentieth century market grew based on the cooperation begun at Bretton Woods. The number of trade agreements increased significantly. In 1960, Iran, Iraq, Kuwait, Saudi Arabia, and Venezuela formed the Organization of the Petroleum Exporting Countries (OPEC). This group coordinates policies and prices in the trade of crude oil. The Asia-Pacific Trade Agreement (APTA) was formed in 1975 to remove trade barriers and promote economic development in Asia and the Pacific. In 1994, the North American Free

Africa on the World Stage

Africa is absent from most discussions about world trade. Although the continent is home to 15 percent of the world's population, Africa supplies only 3 percent of world exports. It consumes the same proportion of world imports. While the standard of living has increased in Asian nations, along with their participation in the world economy, much of Africa remains in poverty.

Africa's small share in the global economy is due to the types of products it sells. While manufactured goods and commercial services make up the majority of the world economy, Africa exports mostly raw materials and agricultural products. Africa's top exports are mineral products, metals, and precious stones. In 2013, Africa supplied 10 percent of world agricultural exports. It provided 66 percent of world fuel and mining exports. But the costs of raw materials, especially fuels, have fallen in recent years. As a result, Africa's export income has suffered. The value of Africa's fuel and mining exports fell by 9 percent in 2013.

However, Africa is also making strides toward participating more in the world market. Africa's exports of merchandise grew by an average of 9 percent a year from 2005 to 2013. In the same time frame, exports of services grew by an average of 6 percent a year. Agricultural exports grew by 5 percent a year. With forty-seven nations in the World Trade Organization (approximately one-third of all WTO members), Africa is working toward a brighter future.

Trade Agreement (NAFTA) lowered tariffs among Canada, the United States, and Mexico.

The flow of goods around the world changed significantly in the twentieth century. In the nineteenth century, nations imported raw materials and primary products or harvested them from their own land. Then the goods were processed in the country and exported as final products. Traded goods were either unprocessed materials or finished manufactured products. By contrast, nations in the twentieth century began to focus production on manufactured parts, or ***components***. These parts are shipped to other factories, often in other countries, for the next stage of assembly. Components and incomplete products may cross national borders many times before the product is complete. Today, components make up approximately one-third of all world trade.

The continued drop in transportation and communication costs helped create today's global supply chains, which are based on component production. International airmail was first used in 1911. Federal Express began promising next-day worldwide delivery in the 1970s. The development of shipping containers also contributed to the frenzied pace of global commerce. These metal crates can transition between trains, trucks, and ships.

The Internet has affected globalization more than any other invention. Buyers, sellers, and producers can exchange information instantly online. Prices of overseas products and materials are a click away. Payments can be sent electronically. Furthermore, international business

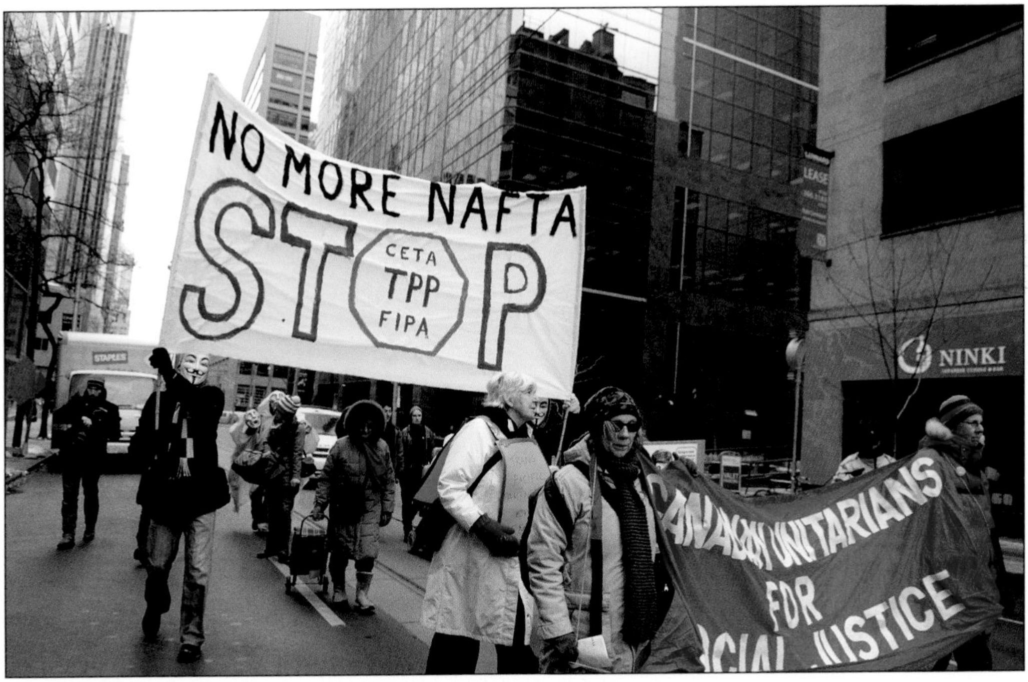

Although free-trade agreements like NAFTA have created economic growth, many people are opposed to them because they fear a loss of jobs to lower-income countries. These Canadians are protesting in Toronto against the proposed Trans-Pacific Partnership Agreement (TPP) in January 2016.

deals can be struck "face-to-face" with videoconferencing. Combined with the previous developments of the computer and the microprocessor, the Internet is a powerful engine of economic growth.

The ease of transportation and communication means that products and parts can be made in the nations with the absolute lowest production costs. For example, US car companies purchase components from all over the world. Factory workers put the parts together to form complete vehicles. The factories may or may not be located in the

Rows of new cars are lined up in port, waiting to be loaded onto cargo ships for export to foreign markets.

United States. This use of products and labor at their cheapest global source is called ***outsourcing***. Outsourcing has moved many manufacturing jobs from Western countries to nations with less expensive labor.

Communication technology has also led to outsourcing of professional services. Today, companies can hire accountants, engineers, and customer service workers in other nations.

Multinational companies and international investment also arose in the twentieth century. Today, companies with operations in more than one nation account for over two-thirds of international trade. And the global market is increasingly driven by funds from overseas. Foreign investment in Canada hit a high mark in 1970. That year 36 percent of investments in nonfinancial industries were controlled by foreigners (mostly Americans).

The twenty-first century brought a new kind of global market. Once, Westerners showed off luxury items from other nations. Today, cheap goods with international origins fill homes and businesses. People even purchase goods from foreign sellers over the Internet instead of driving to the store. In addition, nations are bound together by a complex balance sheet of traded goods and services.

Text-Dependent Questions

1. How did the Bretton Woods system lay the foundation for the global economy of the twentieth century?
2. Describe three differences between globalization in the nineteenth century and globalization in the twentieth century.

Research Project

Find out more about how the World Bank helps developing nations. Select a country that currently has a loan with the World Bank. Research the country's needs and how it is using the World Bank loan to improve its economy. Pay special attention to the development of products and services for export. Then pretend you are a political leader from that country and write a one-page progress report to the World Bank about the success of the loan-funded projects.

Over the past two decades, improvements in trade finance, the Internet, and an increase in the number of free-trade agreements have dramatically increased opportunities for US and Canadian companies to access markets worldwide.

5

Trade in the New Millennium

A lot has changed since the first age of globalization began in the nineteenth century. According to the WTO, "Since the mid-1800s, the world's population has grown roughly six-fold, world output has grown 60-fold, and world trade has grown over 140-fold." In 1870, international trade accounted for 4.6 percent of world GDP. In 1998, goods traded between countries made up 17.2 percent of world income.

In the last thirty years, the global market has grown even faster. From 1980 to 2011, the amount of exported goods rose an average of 7.3 percent each year. This growth received several big boosts at the end of the twentieth century. The breakup of the Soviet Union in 1991 into fifteen individual nations added markets to the world economy. The Internet boom in the 1990s connected foreign markets, created new services, and expanded consumer demand. And, finally, many Asian countries opened to free trade in recent decades. These nations began producing and exporting goods at a feverish pace.

The Big Players

For most of the twentieth century, the United States, Western Europe, and Japan exported the bulk of traded goods. However, the share of ***developing nations*** in the world economy has recently increased. Asian nations like China, Taiwan, South Korea, Malaysia, Singapore, and Thailand have gained major positions in the global market. Their success has resulted from fast income growth and high manufacturing output. Developing countries are now responsible for one-third of all world exports.

Asian participation in the global economy is expanding quickly. China is at the forefront of this growth. The largest country in Asia tripled its share of world exports from 1990 to 2007. China now sells more goods than any other nation.

Words to Understand in This Chapter

developed nations—nations that have strong industries and relatively few poor people.

developing nations—nations with few, but growing industries and a proportion of poor people that is large, but decreasing.

quota—a limit on the amount of things allowed, such as a limit on the amount of a good allowed into a country.

specialization—the act of focusing on only the few goods and services that a nation can produce most cheaply.

subsidy—money the government pays to producers to keep the price of a good or service low.

value-added terms—a method of counting export values so each component of a product is counted only once.

Chinese workers produce electronics equipment in a factory in Shenzhen, a city that has become a center for technology manufacturing.

The expansion of China's industries fuels this growth. The rising skill level of Chinese workers also plays a role. Chinese factories, like the ones that make Apple iPhones, employ scores of highly educated engineers. And they provide jobs for even more workers with mid-level skills. In addition, funds for new factories, production processes, and worker training have become more readily available in China.

By contrast, the United States, Canada, Japan, and Europe make up a smaller proportion of total world exports than they did in the twentieth century. Of course, these *developed nations* still trade on a huge scale. Yet they do not have the top positions of times past. Developing countries, such as Brazil, Russia, India, and China, have become more active in international trade. Thus, they are gaining influence in the global economy and the World Trade Organization.

In fact, these four nations may soon be the most significant participants in the world market. They have already received so much attention that economists have given them a special title. These countries are known as BRIC (spelled from the first letters of their names). Each of the BRIC nations experienced immense growth after switching from closed markets to free trade in the twentieth century. Their combined GDP tripled from 2001 to 2011. In 2012, their total income was $13 trillion. The BRIC nations are also among the top ten most populous countries in the world. Therefore, they supply a large portion of workers and consumers in the world economy. It is likely that the BRIC nations will one day overtake the previous prominence of North America, Europe, and Japan.

The future health of the global market depends on the relationships between the old economic powers—the United States, Europe, and Japan—and the new heavyweights—Brazil, Russia, India, China, and other developing economies. In particular, the relationship between the United States and China is both delicate and critical to stability. A trade war between these nations could cause disaster. A break in the US-China supply chain would lead to widespread unemployment in China and product shortages

A Brazilian steel worker checks a blast furnace at the country's largest steel mill, Usiminas in Minas Gerais.

in the United States. These problems would quickly affect other areas of these nations', and the world's, economies.

A Changing Global Market

The growth of developing nations stems from their focus on the two main areas of global trade: manufactured merchandise and services. In 2008, 45 percent of world exports were services. Manufactured goods accounted for 37 percent of world exports. Raw materials made up only 18 percent of world trade.

Much of trade today is in components. These parts cross multiple national borders as they advance in the global sup-

In 2008, the US stock market fell by 30 percent. As the trouble lingered through 2009, it affected foreign investments in the US market. Other nations suffered and the world economy slowed. The US and Canadian stock markets did not recover to 2008 levels until 2012. World trade began rebounding sooner, although imports and exports have grown at only modest rates of 2 to 3 percent a year since 2010.

ply chain. Therefore, total world exports cannot be accurately counted by adding up the total exports from each country. However, measuring the trade of manufactured goods in ***value-added terms*** counts only the new parts in an exported product. Thus, parts that have already been tallied as exports in other countries are not counted again. For example, suppose a company in Korea makes zippers. It exports the zippers to a Mexican factory that produces backpacks using those zippers. The factory sells the backpacks to a Canadian store. The zippers are not counted again as part of the backpack's value for reporting Mexico's export total.

Asia, in particular, focuses on manufacturing component parts. Asian companies make parts for everything from cars to cell phones to coffeemakers. The component market is the result of ***specialization***. Specialization is the act of focusing production on only the few goods that a nation can make most cheaply. The continued decrease in transportation costs and the decline in trade barriers has allowed goods to move freely between national borders. This movement encourages specialization.

In the twenty-first century, specialization has become the norm. Not only do nations specialize in a category of goods, they often focus on a specific type of product within that category. For example, Germany and Japan both produce automobiles. German companies like BMW, Mercedes-Benz, and Porsche are known for producing luxury cars with high price tags. Japanese auto companies like Toyota, Honda, and Subaru target middle-class buyers who value useful features such as high gas mileage. As a result of this ultra-specialization, nations trade goods from the same category. Wealthy Japanese consumers purchase German luxury cars, while middle-class German consumers purchase Japanese cars.

As the trade of manufactured merchandise increases, so does the trade of services. This is partly because companies that produce products also need packaging designers, webpage managers, and bookkeepers. Companies that sell more goods need more service workers. From 1980 to 2011, the trade in services rose an average of 8.2 percent a year. In fact, services now make up nearly half of all traded goods. This increase is partly due to inexpensive communication costs. In addition, some nations have focused on training in service skills, such as English-language and accounting skills. At present, India is the fastest-growing provider of services. It hosts accounting firms, customer service call centers, and other service centers for many foreign companies. India's large number of educated English speakers and its low wages make the country a prime supplier of services to the wealthy nations of the West.

Controversy in the Global Market

Globalization has improved life for most of the world's 7.3 billion people. The global market connects people with each other. It also provides access to diverse, inexpensive products. Since the Industrial Revolution, the standard of living in most nations has increased. More and more people are making the leap from earning only enough (or less than enough) to cover basic needs to being global consumers.

Yet globalization is not without problems. In the United States, support for international trade has recently declined. Americans are worried about job outsourcing, benefits for the losers in world competition, agricultural ***subsidies***, and global working conditions. In 2002, 78 percent of Americans said that free-trade agreements were good for the country. Only 58 percent agreed with that position in 2015. On the other hand, world trade receives high approval in China and India, two of the world's fastest-growing economies. In 2015, 91 percent of Chinese believed trade benefited their nation. The approval rating was 89 percent in India.

The souring of US attitudes toward global trade is due in large part to the demise of job security. On average, US workers are about 30 percent more likely to lose their jobs than they were two decades ago. And workers earn about 14 percent less when they find new employment. Thus job outsourcing receives a lot of attention in the United States and in other Western countries. Westerners worry about jobs moving from local factories to plants in high-labor, low-wage nations.

> **Did You Know?**
>
> About 40 percent of the world's population lives in Brazil, Russia, India, and China. In 2016, the combined population of the BRIC nations was more than 3 billion people.

Job loss in Western countries leads to another debate. Should the government compensate people who lose income as a result of global competition? After World War II, social welfare programs were put in place to help citizens who lost out to free trade. Most Western countries now have these programs. The idea is that because the nation as a whole benefits from free trade, the whole nation should compensate globalization's losers with tax-funded programs. Today, unemployment insurance and reeducation programs attempt to soften the blow of world competition. By making up for the damage globalization causes, these programs promote public support for participation in the world market.

Another debate related to outsourcing concerns working conditions around the world. Some people argue that the cost savings of using workers in other countries are not justified because the workers there are not treated fairly. Westerners, in particular, hold values about the quality of work life. These concerns include how many hours per day and per week an employee should be required to work, the amount of paid break time workers should receive, the cleanliness of workplaces, and fair wages for specific jobs. Some of the workplaces in Asia, the Middle East, and South America do not meet Westerners' expectations on these issues.

Another controversial topic is protection for agriculture. While trade barriers for other goods have shrunk, nations share a reservation about allowing the free movement of agricultural goods. The United States pays farmers $8 billion in subsidies per year. These government payments allow farmers to sell their crops for artificially low rates. Low prices make US products cheaper than products from other nations. Countries also drive up the prices of imported agricultural goods with ***quotas***. Quotas cap the amount of goods allowed to enter a country. The GATT discussions that started in Doha, Qatar in 2001 aimed to end agricultural subsidies. But the negotiations stalled. All nations hesitated to strip protections from farmers.

Tomorrow's Global Market

Based on the overall growth of the global market in the past two hundred years, it is nearly certain that globalization will persist in the near future. Many current trends will also likely continue. Asian production, especially in China, will increase. However, Asia's future growth may be slower than it was over the last twenty years. Likewise, the share in world exports among developing nations will keep rising. North America's and Europe's shares will likely decrease, although the WTO predicts that the United States will hold its ground.

It's also probable that global supply chains will continue to grow more complex. And products will move even more freely across borders. In addition, the trade of services will probably keep rising. The increase in international trade relationships and the reduction of trade barriers will also promote growth. And, as technology moves forward, it will connect even more people to the world market.

The global market is here to stay. While disturbances will occasionally ripple through the globe, the basic structure of free trade in the world economy will remain. With the help of the World Trade Organization and other international coalitions, trade will increase and people's lives will improve.

Text-Dependent Questions

1. Name five developing countries that are gaining influence in the global market.
2. List three reasons for the increase in the trade of services in the twenty-first century.

Research Project

Create a bar graph on graph paper or a computer that shows the trade activity of the ten most populous nations. For each country, represent the value in US dollars of exported goods, imported goods, exported services, and imported services. Be sure to use recent data from the same year for all nations. Title your graph and label each bar and the x- and y-axes.

Organizations to Contact

Department of Foreign Affairs, Trade and Development (Canada)
125 Sussex Drive
Ottawa, ON K1A 0G2
Canada
Phone: (800) 267-8376
Fax: (613) 996-9709
Website: www.international.gc.ca/

International Economic History Association (IEHA)
McClelland Hall, 401GG
P.O. Box 210108
Tucson, AZ 85721-0108
Phone: (520) 621-4421
Fax: (520) 621-8450
Email: fishback@email.arizona.edu
Website: www.eh.net/EHA

Organisation for Economic Co-operation and Development (OECD)
Washington Centre
2001 L Street, NW, Suite 650,
Washington, DC 20036-4922
Phone: (202) 785-6323
Fax: (202) 785-0350
E-mail: washington.contact@oecd.org
Website: www.oecd.org

US Chamber of Commerce
1615 H Street, NW
Washington, DC 20062
Phone: (202) 659-6000
Fax: (202) 463-3126
Email: Americas@uschamber.com
Website: www.uschamber.com

World Trade Organization (WTO)
Centre William Rappard
Rue de Lausanne 154
CH-1211 Geneva 21
Switzerland
Phone: +41 (0)22 739-5111
Fax: +41 (0)22 731-4206
Email: enquiries@wto.org
Website: www.wto.org

EISENMANN
EISENMANN
Eurostyle
4

Series Glossary

barter—the official department that administers and collects the duties levied by a government on imported goods.

bond—a debt investment used by companies and national, state, or local governments to raise money to finance projects and activities. The corporation or government borrows money for a defined period of time at a variable or fixed interest rate.

credit—the ability of a customer to obtain goods or services before payment, based on the trust that payment will be made in the future.

customs—the official department that administers and collects the duties or tariffs levied by a government on imported goods.

debt—money, or something else, that is owed or due in exchange for goods or services.

demurrage—extra charges paid to a ship or aircraft owner when a specified period for loading or unloading freight has been exceeded.

distributor—a wholesaler or middleman engaged in the distribution of a category of goods, esp to retailers in a specific area.

duty—a tax on imported goods.

export—to send goods or services to another country for sale.

Federal Reserve—the central bank of the United States, which controls the amount of money circulating in the US economy and helps to set interest rates for commercial banks.

import—to bring goods or services into a country from abroad for sale.

interest—a fee that is paid in exchange for the use of money that has been borrowed, or for delaying the repayment of a debt.

stock—an ownership interest in a company. Stocks are sold by companies to raise money for their operations. The price of a successful company's stock will typically rise, which means the person who originally bought the stock can sell it and earn a profit.

tariff—a government-imposed tax that must be paid on certain imported or exported goods.

value added tax (VAT)—a type of consumption tax that is placed on a product whenever value is added at each stage of production and at final sale. VAT is often used in the European Union.

World Bank—an international financial organization, connected to the United Nations. It is the largest source of financial aid to developing countries.

Further Reading

Aronson, Marc, and Marina Budhos. *Sugar Changed the World: A Story of Magic, Spice, Slavery, Freedom, and Science*. Boston: Clarion, 2010.

Bailey, Diane. *How Markets Work*. New York: Rosen Publishing, 2011.

Crayton, Lisa. *Globalization: What It Is and How It Works*. New York: Enslow, 2016.

Dee, Megan. *The European Union in a Multipolar World: World Trade, Global Governance and the Case of the WTO*. New York: Macmillan, 2015.

Mann, Charles, and Rebecca Stefoff. *1493 for Young People: From Columbus's Voyage to Globalization*. New York: Triangle Square, 2016.

Matthews, Sheelagh. *Trade and Global Impact*. Calgary, Alberta, Canada: Weigl, 2010.

Reis, Ronald. *The World Trade Organization*. New York: Chelsea House, 2009.

Internet Resources

www.econlib.org/index.html

The Library of Economics and Liberty website hosts an economic encyclopedia, a library of articles written by economics scholars, podcasts, and other resources related to a variety of economics topics, including international trade and globalization.

www.econedlink.org/student/

This website, hosted by the Council for Economic Education, has resources and lessons on a variety of economic topics, including world trade. Learn more about trade barriers, currency exchange markets, and transportation's role in the economy.

www.cia.gov/library/publications/the-world-factbook/

The World Factbook is a resource of the US Central Intelligence Agency (CIA). This online encyclopedia gives information on each nation, including import, export, and foreign investment data.

www.wto.org/english/forums_e/students_e/students_e.htm

The World Trade Organization's website for students includes articles and videos about the WTO and the world economy.

Publisher's Note: The websites listed on this page were active at the time of publication. The publisher is not responsible for websites that have changed their address or discontinued operation since the date of publication. The publisher reviews and updates the websites each time the book is reprinted.

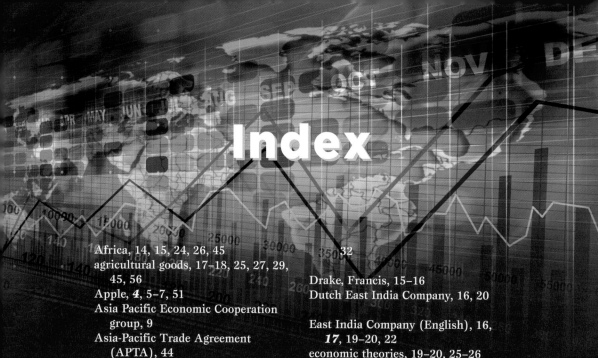

Index

Numbers in ***bold italic*** refer to captions.

About the Author

Laura Helweg is an editor at the University of Kansas. For fun, she writes about history and culture for children and teens. She is the author of *Eastern Great Lakes: Indiana, Michigan, Ohio* (Mason Crest, 2015) and many magazine articles. Laura lives in Lawrence, Kansas with her best friend and husband, Michael, and their orange tabby cat, Linus. Laura likes to read books about historical heroes, play the drums, and cook meals from around the world.

Picture Credits: Everett Historical: 37, 41; Library of Congress: 21, 28 (right); National Archives: 44; Photos.com, a division of Getty Images: 32; used under license from Shutterstock, Inc.: 2, 11, 16, 25, 28, 46, 51, 58, 64, 79; Arindam Banerjee / Shutterstock.com: 55; Canadapanda / Shutterstock.com: 6; Toni Genes / Shutterstock.com: 14; Andrei Kholmov / Shutterstock.com: 71; Bartlomiej Magierowski / Shutterstock.com: 61; Nui7711 / Shutterstock.com: 12; StockStudio / Shutterstock.com: 56; T photography / Shutterstock.com: 63; United Nations photo: 49.